My First Book about the Alphabet of Pets

Amazing Animal Books
Children's Picture Books

By Molly Davidson

Mendon Cottage Books

JD-Biz Publishing

Download Free Books!
http://MendonCottageBooks.com

Read More Amazing Animal Books

Purchase at Amazon.com

Download Free Books!
http://MendonCottageBooks.com

Introduction

In the United States, about 65% of all households own at least one pet, and 42% own more than one pet.

Freshwater fish is the number one pet, in the United States.

A is for an Abyssinian.

The Abyssinian cat breed has been around since ancient Egyptian time, when they were sold as pets on the bank of the Nile River.

They are very smart, playful, and active, they usually don't just sit.

 **is for a Betta Fish.**

Betta fish are also called Siamese fighting fish; this is why they need to be in their own tank.

They eat meat, like bloodworms, shrimp, crickets, flies, and grasshoppers.

C is for a Chinchilla.

Chinchillas run wild in the Andes Mountains of South America.

In 1920, the first chinchillas were made pets in California.

They live between 10 - 18 years.

C is also for Chickens.

Chickens have been pets for over 10,000 years.

The Indians were the first to own them; they used them for eggs, feathers, and meat.

There are over 25 billion chickens in the World, which is more than any other bird.

D is for a Dachshund.

Dachshund dogs are very playful and love to chase birds, tennis balls, and small animals.

They have a loud bark, so they are a great watchdog.

They are very loyal to their owners, but maybe shy around strangers.

E is for Equus Caballus, the scientific name for a horse.

There're over 4.8 million pet horses in the U.S.

Horses eat grass and plants, and live for about 30 years.

They have a blind spot right behind them and right in front of their nose, so always come up to a horse from the side.

is for a Ferret.

Ferrets were first had as a pet over 2,500 years ago, and would help farmers hunt rabbits.

They sleep for 6 hours at a time before waking up to play and eat; in total they sleep about 18 hours per day.

G is for Goldfish.

A school (group) of goldfish is called a troubling.

Goldfish don't have eyelids, so they don't blink and they sleep with their eyes open.

They have teeth in their throat which helps them crush their food.

G is for also for Guinea Pigs.

Guinea pigs only grow to be about one foot (30 cm) long.

They can live up to 7 years, if kept as a pet.

Over 7,000 years ago they were eaten as food.

 is for a Hamster.

Hamsters make a great first pet, because they are quiet, small, and calm.

They like to live by themselves, not with other hamsters, and live for about 2 - 3 years.

They store food in their cheeks, so they can store it in their burrow later.

 **is also for a Hermit Crab.**

Hermit crabs have a soft body that is protected by its shell, as it grows it will need larger shells.

I is for an Iguana.

Iguanas are found in the jungles of Central and South America; they are also the 7th most popular pet in America.

They will change their skin color depending on their mood.

 is for a Javanese Cat.

Nickolas Titkov © <u>Wikimedia Commons</u>

Javanese cats are a long haired mixture of Siamese and Balinese cats.

They are pretty quiet cats, but they do have opinions and will let you know when they need something.

 **is for Koi.**

Koi are very popular pets in Japan, because they believe they symbolize wealth, prosperity, love, successful career, and good fortune.

L is for a Labrador Retriever.

Labrador retrievers are the number one dog kept as a pet.

They are great at retrieving (fetching) objects; they are widely used as hunting dogs.

They are very gentle and can even carry an egg in their mouth without breaking it.

M is for a Mouse.

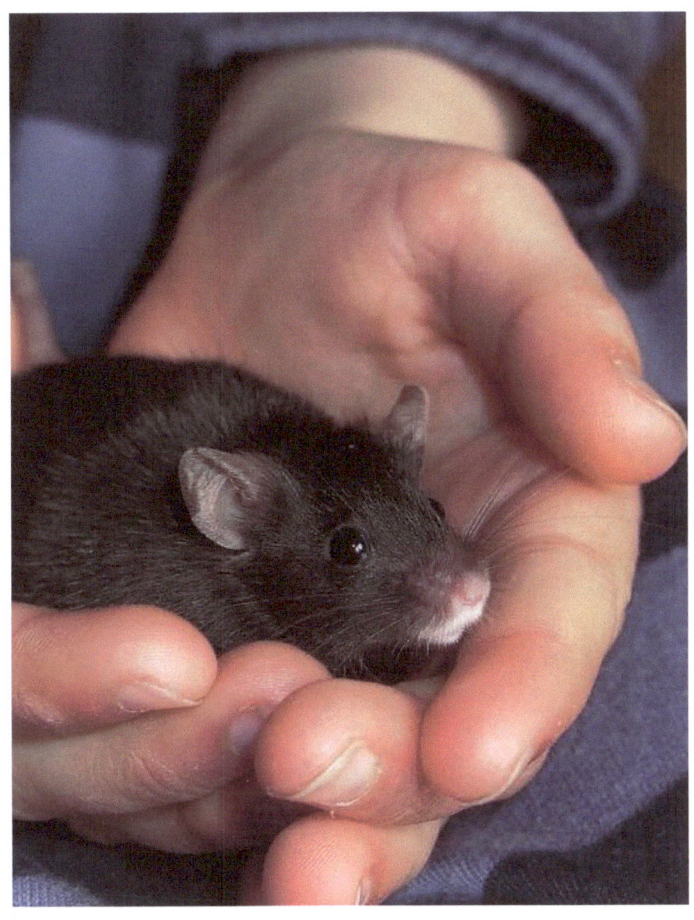

Mice are the 5th most popular pet, because they are small, cuddly, and are found everywhere in the World.

 **is for a Norwegian Forest Cat.**

Norwegian forest cats are popular pets in the colder regions, because they have two thick layers of fur, which help keep them warm.

 **is for an Oriental Cat.**

Oriental cats are very talkative and need other cats to help keep them happy.

They are smart, athletic, quick, and playful.

They can be more than 300 different colors and patterns.

P is for a Parrot.

Birds are the number 4 most popular pet, and parrots are the most popular bird, since there are over 350 different species

Parrots can live for up to 60 years.

They use their sharp beaks to eat nuts and berries.

Q is for a Quail.

Quail can be kept as a pet, just like chickens, outside in a coop.

They are used for their mini spotted eggs and to eat for meat.

 **is for a Rabbit.**

Rabbits are the 5th most popular pet in the U.S., since they are quiet, small, and fuzzy.

They love to eat grass, and always need to have something to chew on to keep their teeth from growing too long.

 **is for Snakes.**

Snakes like to live by themselves, so be sure to have only one per cage.

Be careful choosing a pet snake, they can bite and carry salmonella, which can make you ill.

T is for a Turtle.

Turtles have lived on the Earth since the time of dinosaurs.

They are one of the top 10 best pets.

Their shells are made up of more than 60 bones connected together.

 **is for a Weasel.**

Weasels can be great pets, if you want them for hunting small animals.

Many farmers do not like them, because they try to eat the baby livestock.

Baby weasels only take 5 weeks to be born and are called kittens.

X 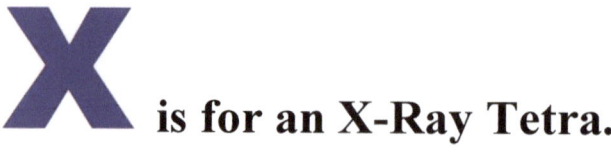 is for an X-Ray Tetra.

X-Ray Tetras' have clear scales so you can see their back bone, like an x-ray.

They are happy to share their tank with many other kinds of fish, they are very peaceful.

They are one of the most popular tropical fish to have as pets in your tank.

 **is for a Yellow - Crested Cockatoo.**

Yellow - Crested Cockatoos eat lots of fresh fruit, vegetables, and nuts.

They're very playful; they need toys and 3 - 4 hours of playtime, out of their cage, per day.

Conclusion

I hope you have enjoyed reading about many exciting pets.

One more interesting fact, one of the most popular pets in Asia is crickets!

Download Free Books!

http://MendonCottageBooks.com

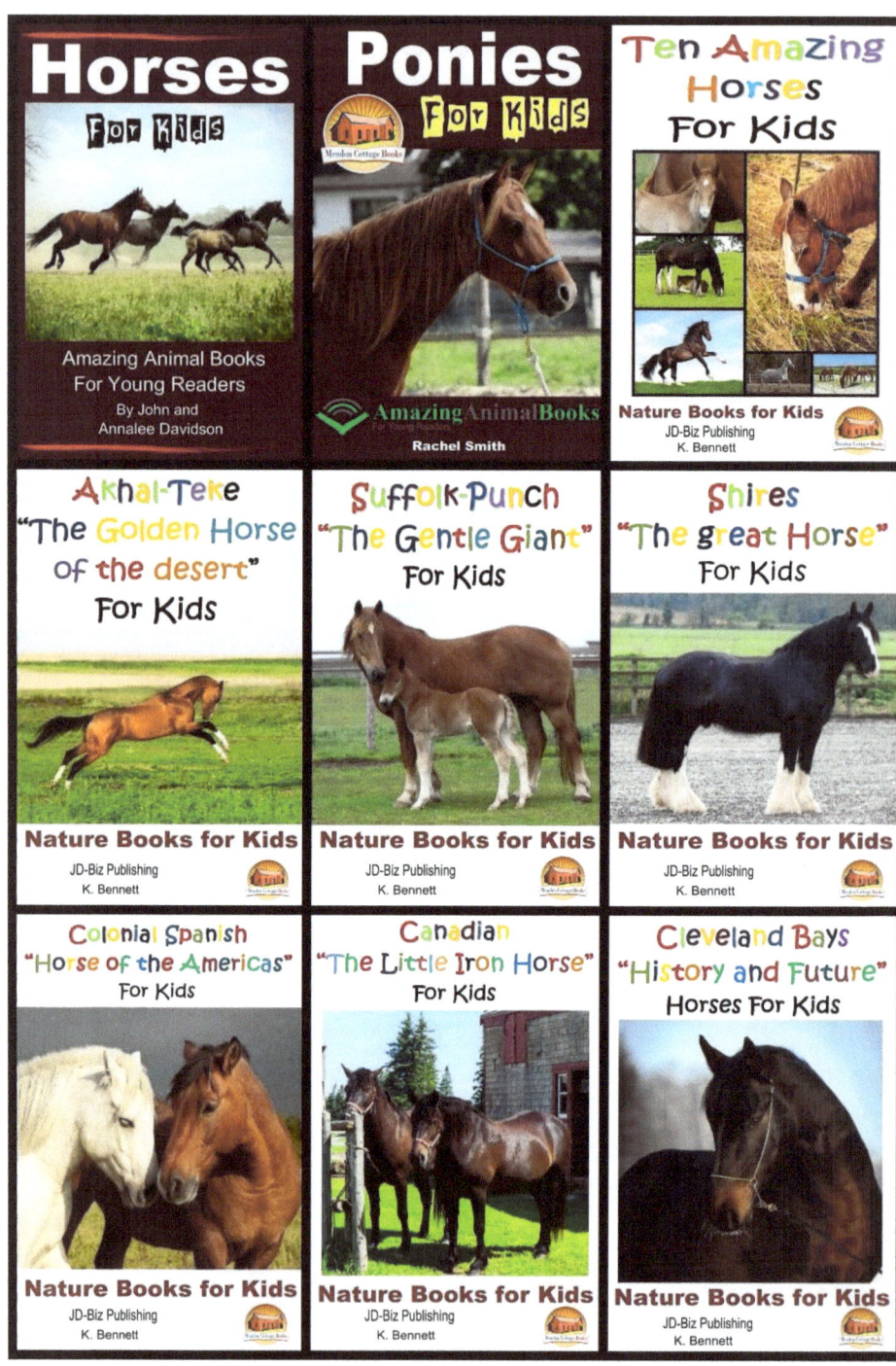

Our books are available at

1. Amazon.com

2. Barnes and Noble

3. Itunes

4. Kobo

5. Smashwords

6. Google Play Books

Download Free Books!
http://MendonCottageBooks.com

Publisher

JD-Biz Corp

P O Box 374

Mendon, Utah 84325

http://www.jd-biz.com/

www.ingramcontent.com/pod-product-compliance
Lightning Source LLC
Chambersburg PA
CBHW050902290526
45792CB00002B/677